ORGANIC GARDENING TIPS & GUIDES

For Beginners

(Beginners Guide to Growing Your Own Organic Vegetables, Fruits, and Plants)

By

ANN WILLIVAN

Copyright

© 2021 Ann Willivan

All rights reserved

No part of this book may be reproduced, store in a retrieval device, or transmitted by any means without the adequate consent and permission of the publisher.

Contact:

bornlandltd@gmail.com

TABLE OF CONTENT

Copyright

TABLE OF CONTENT

INTRODUCTION

CHAPTER 1

ORGANIC GARDENING CONCEPT

CHAPTER 2

WHY GROW ORGANICALLY?

CHAPTER 3

ORGANIC GARDENING SUPPLIES

CHAPTER 4

DECIDING WHAT TO GROW

CHAPTER 5

PLANTING YOUR VEGETABLE GARDEN

CHAPTER 6

MAKING YOUR GARDEN THRIVE

CHAPTER 7

HANDLING YOUR ORGANIC VEGETABLES

CHAPTER 8

HOW TO HARVEST ORGANIC VEGETABLES

CHAPTER 9

HOW TO STORE YOUR ORGANIC VEGETABLES

CONCLUSION

INTRODUCTION

A nice book you cannot afford to miss. Get ready to acquire the best knowledge for organic gardening.

The information in this book will enlighten you about the best Organic Gardening method that works perfectly. Organic gardening isn't as difficult as many first-time gardeners believe. It is true that an organic garden requires a little more work and more attention to detail than a regular garden. However, with the right guidance, you'll soon realize it's not nearly as difficult as you thought. This guide will walk you through the fundamental steps required to get started.

Let's assume you know nothing about organic gardening, this book will teach you what you need to know about Organic gardening. Simply put, it means that you will plant your garden without using synthetic fertilizers to help the plants grow or chemical pesticides to keep the bugs at bay.

It's best to have a detailed plan for your garden, whether it's going to be flowers, herbs, vegetables, or a mishmash of several plants. And the best time to make your plan is in the fall, just as the growing season is coming to an end. This is because you'll have more time to prepare the ground before the spring planting season starts.

The most important thing you can do before anything else is to choose the best location for your organic garden, or any garden for that matter. If you can give your plants about six hours of sunlight per day, they will thrive. In almost all cases, placing your planting area in the southeast corner of your yard will provide more than enough sunlight. Also, ensure that your ground has easy access to water and adequate drainage to allow for water runoff and aeration.

After the correct location has been determined, the next step is to prepare the land for planting. This means it's time to do some physical labor. You will plow the soil with a garden fork or field cultivator, then kneel down to pull out weeds, grass and stones. To successfully remove weeds and grasses, you must remove them first, and then come back a few weeks later to remove all weeds and grasses that have grown during this period.

Now is the time for you to really determine what is needed in the process of getting the proper nutrients in the selected area to help the vegetation grow. The soil needs to be checked for proper landscaping. Do some precise work and take the soil samples to your local nursery or garden center and they can do it for you. After nursery workers complete the test, they can tell you which type of natural fertilization and pest control to use in the nursery or garden center to get advice on which plants and vegetables will thrive in the soil you are dealing with.

Read this guide attentively. This guide will provide you with the fundamentals you'll need to get your organic gardening project off on the right foot. It covered the garden's location, sunlight exposure, ground preparation prior to planting, and the proper nutrition your soil will require. Organic gardening isn't as difficult as it appears. You will learn more about Organic Gardening as you read this book to the end.

CHAPTER 1
ORGANIC GARDENING CONCEPT

Home gardens have been sitting back to other outdoor hobbies for many years. Gardening at home in recent generations has become old-fashioned and a waste of time, because in any local food store, vegetables and produce can be bought. Yet younger people are concerned about the rural life and healthier diets as the economy has changed. More attention was paid to home gardening and organic gardening with this interest.

Food shops have begun to deliver organic vegetables, but many shoppers have noticed that organic vegetables often are much more costly than non-organic. This prevents shoppers from organically buying and eating on a tight budget. The alternative is to spend large sums on organic vegetables. People can now grow their own organic food, not buy it irrespective of their living situation or gardening spaces.

A small balcony can grow many great organic vegetables so you don't need to start to grow organic vegetables in your own home and garden.

This book was specially created for those of you who are interested but who don't know where or how to begin growing organic vegetables at home. It will help you to easily and affordably establish your own garden now, with a detailed, easy to understand and guide designed to help you start your own organic vegetable garden quicker than you would have expected.

If you're a little afraid to start your own organic vegetable garden, or generally do not worry about gardening! It's much easier to start a home garden than many people can even understand, even if you've never seen a farm or home or garden before. Organic gardening is just as easy, as many people and farmers do today. It's a more natural approach to gardening. You can start your garden small to get comfortable with organic crops and add to it over time.

You'll be amazed at how simple it is to start your own organic vegetable garden with the help of this book, and you'll wonder why you didn't start your own garden years ago.

You'll be able to grow nutritious vegetables for yourself, your friends, and your family. You will learn how to harvest organic vegetables as well as how to store them once harvested. Starting an organic garden will give you an excuse to spend a few minutes each day outside monitoring your growing garden and enjoying the weather.

Organic gardening can even become a family pastime. People of all ages can enjoy and benefit from growing organic vegetables. You will be glad you did

CHAPTER 2
WHY GROW ORGANICALLY?

Many first-time gardeners may be perplexed as to why they should bother planting organic vegetables. They wonder whether it makes any long-term difference. A person must understand first what organic gardening really is before this question can be answered.

Organic gardening consists of gardening without the use of chemical fertilizers or pesticides. The soil in which plants are planted is used in most gardens that have bought fertilizers that are packed with chemicals. Later on, more pesticides and weed killers are purchased in the store while the insects and weeds that are included in any garden are being sprinkled into the vegetables.

Many people believe that using store-bought fertilizers, weed killers, and pesticides is the best option. It's often thought to be easier to run to the store, buy a bottle of "weed killer," and spray your garden whenever weeds appear. When pests appear or the vegetables do not appear to be growing well, the process is repeated. The issue with using these chemically enhanced store-bought items is that you never know what you're exposing your vegetables to until it is fully discovered.

Some people do check the ingredients on their products before purchasing them, but the majority of us do not. In fact, many of us are only interested in the cheapest options. We then expose ourselves to potentially harmful chemicals by using them on the food we intend to eat later after purchasing based on price. Yes, most vegetables are washed before being eaten, but how thoroughly and how will washing help when the food was grown with unknown chemical fertilizer? The following are two commonly used pesticides for gardening, as well as their major side effects. Consider the following pesticides attentively:

Malathion

It is important to know that Malathion can cause abdominal pain, stomach cramps, anxiety, shakiness, uncertainty, depressive symptoms, indigestion, breathing difficulty, dizziness, sweating, loss of bowel or bladder control, eyelid, face, and neck twitching, unexpected weakness, and irregular heartbeats.

Skoot

causes headaches, dizziness, memory loss, kidney pain, insomnia, nausea, and vomiting.

All these are two pesticides that can have serious health consequences. There are numerous insecticides and pesticides used on vegetables that have extremely negative side effects. In addition to chemically saturated pesticides, most vegetables are grown with chemically saturated fertilizers, and the vegetable plants are also treated with weed killers, exposing vegetables to even more chemicals than it should.

If you practice the method of growing organically, you give yourself complete control over what goes into the food you eat and eliminate the possibility of pesticide poisoning.

Truly, when you grow vegetables organically, you don't have to worry about what kind of chemicals your vegetables have been exposed to because you know you didn't use any store-bought, man-made chemicals in your garden.

If you believe your vegetable garden requires pesticide or fertilizer, there are natural ways to make both fertilizer and pesticide that do not require the purchase of outside products. It works in a very amazing way.

Organic vegetable gardening, in addition to avoiding the use of pesticides, is a great way to save money and valuable resources. Surprisingly, many gardeners and those interested in starting their own gardens are unaware that starting an organic garden saves money. It's easy to forget that if you don't use store-bought chemicals, you don't have to pay extra money each month for chemicals that you'll quickly outgrow and have to replace. Organic vegetable gardening is a great means of growing valuable needs.

Interestingly, an organic garden can save you lots of money. Yes, it can. If you don't believe that organic gardening will save you money, compare the prices of store-bought fertilizers, pesticides, and even weed killers the next time you go shopping. Imagine having to buy the cheapest items on a regular basis to keep your garden going on top of your regular household groceries and supplies.

Consider how much money you will save if you avoid using these expensive products entirely.

Consider how much money you will save by not having to waste gas on last-minute trips to the store when you realize you are out of these supplies. You can't afford to waste important resources.

Most times, last-minute grocery trips occur more frequently than you realize if you start a garden with chemicals. It is easy to forget to buy weed killer during a hectic grocery store trip, only to return home to find that weeds have taken over your garden. The same thing frequently occurs with pesticides. Many gardeners will not buy a new bottle of pesticide because they haven't seen any insects. Then, all of a sudden, their garden is overrun with hungry insects, destroying the fruits of their labor. Try and prevent the insects from destroying the fruit.

Saving money is a primary concern for you or your family. Therefore, it is necessary to consider the health benefits of organic gardening. Organic vegetables are typically recommended with many diets, particularly those that encourage detoxification and system cleansing.

Keeping a fresh supply of organic vegetables on hand at all times will help you and your family live a healthier lifestyle and will make any organic vegetable detox diet easier to follow.

A detox regiment and organic vegetables can perform wonders for your family's health and health. Many people who eat meals that contain at least 60% organic vegetables report feeling more energized as a result of getting more vitamins and minerals from a natural source. Those who eat a diet high in organic vegetables will see their blood pressure and cholesterol levels drop over time. They'll also have an easier time losing weight because they'll be eating less fat and processed foods. This is very essential needs to be observed.

Organic vegetables taste far better than those heavily processed with chemicals. Well-administered organic vegetables never sprayed with pesticides and other chemicals will usually have a greater taste and flavor than their non-organic counterpart. People eating organic vegetables taste the vegetables rather than the chemicals used to protect and grow their vegetables. Many people who produce organic vegetables do this for the sake of the greatest taste.

CHAPTER 3
ORGANIC GARDENING SUPPLIES

You've learned why you should grow your vegetables organically, and you're probably wondering how to go about doing it.

Starting an organic garden is easier than you might think, especially since you won't have to worry about stocking up on costly, potentially dangerous chemical fertilizers and other supplies. The majority of the items you'll need to start your organic garden are either already in your home or are simple to obtain.

Make sure you plan ahead of time and don't just go out and buy some seeds or plants and begin digging up your yard. That piece of advice will almost certainly be repeated in this book because it is the most common error made by new gardeners.

To have a successful organic garden, you must take your time and carefully plan everything out.

1) **Space**: You'll need a place to plant your organic vegetables before you can start growing them.

This decision will be largely influenced by your living situation. You should consider using pots if you live in a townhouse, apartment, or even a house without a suitable yard. Many small vegetables can be grown in a variety of pots or containers, which come in a variety of sizes.

If you don't have any suitable pots or containers for growing plants, you can order them online for surprisingly low prices or pick them up at your local nursery. Before you spend your money, take a look around your house. You might be surprised to discover that you already have several suitable items or old plant pots on hand.

If you live in a house with a large yard, you will have more options. You can begin your organic garden in any location that you believe is suitable for plant growth. When deciding where to grow organic vegetables in your yard, keep in mind that you want to choose a spot that will receive plenty of sunlight throughout the day.

Finding the best spot for your organic vegetable garden based on lighting will take a few days of careful observation, but it will be well worth it if you can find a suitable location.

The surface area of your organic vegetable garden is entirely up to you and is determined by the amount of space you have available. Don't be afraid to start small and work your way up to a larger garden, and don't be discouraged if you don't have as much space as you'd like for your new garden. You're just getting started and working with the resources you have right now.

1) Soil: The second thing you'll need to get your organic vegetable garden started is good soil, and it's probably the most important aspect of your new garden. If you want your vegetables to grow healthy and strong, the soil you choose must be rich and fertile. Do not give up hope if the soil in your garden appears to be thin or unsuitable. In just a moment, I'll explain how to make the available soil more fertile and ideal for gardening.

Remember that in your new organic vegetable garden, you must not use any chemical fertilizer.

When inspecting the quality of their available soil, most new organic vegetable growers are tempted to use chemicals. If your soil does not appear to be rich enough, it is tempting to go out and buy a bag of soil that is loaded with chemical fertilizers. This is a huge step backward that must be avoided at all costs. There are alternatives to using expensive, and sometimes hazardous, outside chemicals to make your soil rich and suitable for growing.

Getting soil may take a little more effort if you're growing your plants in pots or organic containers on a back patio or window sill. Soil can be obtained from willing neighbors or family members who have yards of their own. Simply request soil and shovel it into your ready-to-use container.

If you don't have access to a garden, consider buying organic soil from a garden supply store. There are some places that sell soil that hasn't had any chemical fertilizers added to it. This may be an additional start-up cost for those who do not have their own backyards, but it will be worthwhile.

You will be able to fill your pots and containers with your own organic soil and then plant your seeds whenever it is convenient for you. Another advantage of using pots and containers is that the temperature of your soil will not be affected by the temperature of the ground.

2) Compost: You'll need this to help your garden thrive, especially if your soil isn't as fertile as you'd like it to be. During the growing seasons, rich compost will provide your soil with the minerals it needs to help your vegetables grow and thrive. Composting is simple to do with materials you already have on hand, especially if you have a backyard or access to an outdoor environment.

To make your own organic compost, start by digging a pit or two in your backyard (depending on the size of your garden).

Fill your pit with the following garbage from your kitchen once it's been dug:

Peeled Vegetables

Leaves

Leaves

Needles

Bark

Shells of Eggs

Coffee Grinds

Stalks of corn

For a while, any fruits, vegetables, and other items mentioned should go into your compost pit instead of the trash. You can also put any leaves you find in the compost pit.

You can also ask your neighbors for their trash to help fill your pits faster. This is especially recommended if you are a single person or a couple who does not generate a lot of trash. Many neighbors will share their trash if they are promised a portion of the fresh harvest when it becomes available.

This compost pile must be started well in advance of the planting season. Starting your compost pit at least three weeks before you plan to start planting seeds, if not sooner, is recommended. The longer your compost ages, the better, so get started on your pit as soon as possible.

As soon as the ground softens enough to work after the winter, you might want to consider digging your compost pit. This way, when it's time to start digging your garden or preparing your containers, your compost will be ready.

If you're growing organic vegetables in a small space with pots and containers, organic compost from a gardening supply store might be a good option. This will be less difficult than trying to make compost in a small space. When working with a limited amount of space, purchasing your own aged compost will be easier and more convenient.

1) Organic Mulch & Newspaper: Anyone starting a new organic vegetable garden should have old newspapers and organic mulch on hand. Organic mulch can be made from a wide range of items found on or near your property. Mulch can be made from fallen leaves, flower blossoms, twigs, tree needles, and even bark.

Mulch is often overlooked by gardeners for reasons other than aesthetics. While mulch will help keep your planted garden looking neater, it also has a number of other advantages that make it an important part of your vegetable garden. For starters, organic mulch will help to prevent weeds from taking over your new garden.

In your vegetable garden, organic mulch will also help to improve the soil quality. Organic mulch, unlike non-organic mulches, will decompose and decay over time, forming a layer of rich and fertile topsoil. In addition to its other benefits, this will provide nutrients to the vegetables.

Before the organic mulch decomposes, it will assist in preventing the water used to water your new vegetable garden from evaporating before it can do its job. It will also assist in maintaining the temperature of your soil by warming it in the winter and cooling it in the summer. This is a fantastic feature for year-round vegetable growers. Another function of the old newspaper is to aid in the growth of your vegetable garden.

You should have a good supply of old newspapers on hand when you're ready to start laying down mulch to protect your newly planted vegetable garden. Before you lay down your mulch, place these newspapers on the ground. The newspaper will help to protect your organic vegetable garden from insects attracted to the mulch.

When selecting mulch and laying it down in and around your garden, there are a few things to keep in mind. For starters, hay should not be used as an organic vegetable garden mulch. Even though hay is readily available and inexpensive in many areas, it is frequently contaminated with weed seed. You'll be contributing to the problem you're trying to avoid.

Make sure the mulch is not too thickly applied. Mulch should be no more than two to three inches thick, and even after it's been laid down, you should keep an eye on it. Check to see if the mulch is matting together, as this could prevent water from reaching your vegetable seeds. Slimy mulch, which occurs when some of the materials used to create a layer of mulch become slimy as they decay, is another thing to keep an eye out for. Simply remove the slimy mulch and replace it with a fresh layer of organic mulch if this occurs.

2) Gloves, Shovels, and Hoes: Other than seed, you'll only need a few old-fashioned garden tools to get your garden started, and if you don't already have them, you can buy them anywhere that sells gardening supplies. To dig your compost pits and garden area, you'll need a good shovel. For any weeding that needs to be done, a good garden hoe and a good pair of strong gloves will be required.

When shoveling and doing more hands-on garden work, you'll need gloves to protect your hands. Weeding, in particular, will necessitate a good pair of gloves, as pulling weeds up by hand rather than using a hoe to kill them will often be easier.

CHAPTER 4
DECIDING WHAT TO GROW

When you've gathered all of the materials necessary to establish and maintain an organic vegetable garden, you'll need something to put in it. For many, choosing which vegetables to plant is the most enjoyable aspect because it allows them to imagine the variety of crops that will sprout from their new garden.

Numerous retailers, both online and offline, sell organic vegetable seeds. Indeed, there are so many seeds available that some people become absolutely overwhelmed by the variety.

If you have never grown vegetables before, it is necessary that you stick to easy-to-grow crops. Even if these are vegetables you have never eaten or considered growing, you may be surprised by the outcomes.

Numerous organic gardeners have discovered that vegetables they previously despised when purchased canned or frozen tasted lovely when grown in their own backyard. Here are a few vegetables that are simple to organically grow and frequently make for a delectable treat.

<u>Tomatoes</u>

Many people know that tomatoes are an important vegetable to cultivate at home due to their ability to thrive in a variety of temperatures. There are numerous tomatoes cultivars, many of which do not require stakes or fences to grow against. Cherry tomatoes are particularly popular because they are typically pricey in supermarkets but are excellent in salads and as an appetizer in a variety of recipes.

There are things you need to do to ensure your tomatoes grow well. When planting organic tomatoes, it is necessary that they receive enough amount of water and sunlight. To ensure the greatest outcomes and the largest yield possible, harvest your tomatoes as soon as they begin to ripe.

Chilies & Peppers

Nutritionists have confirmed that peppers are an excellent organic vegetable to cultivate if you have limited space or want to grow vegetables in pots or jars. They will flourish and grow nearly all year if the conditions are favorable. Peppers do not have to be harvested immediately upon appearance of ripeness. This allows you to plan ahead and harvest your peppers as needed.

After harvesting all of your peppers, storing is simple. They can be dried by keeping them in a dark, dry, well-ventilated area (such as an attic) for many weeks. If you do not have a suitable location for drying peppers and chilies, they will frequently keep for several months if stored in a well-sealed glass jar.

Zucchini

Zucchini and the majority of squash/pumpkins are excellent for beginning organic gardeners. They are simple to plant and develop quickly, which means you will not have to wait extended periods of time to see results. Many individuals believe that their zucchinis grow overnight.

While growing zucchini and other squash, it is imperative to know that you or a member of your family pick them immediately. This will aid in the growth of new plants and provide you with a bountiful harvest. However, if you are cultivating pumpkins, you must wait until all of the vines have died before harvesting.

Peas

If you have tasted peas, you will testify that it is very nice. Peas are a favorite vegetable of many children, making them an excellent choice for growing food for a family. Peas are another food that will grow in enormous quantities throughout the spring, summer, and even into the winter. Peas grow virtually all year in some locations, giving them an excellent source of fresh, organic food.

The moment you begin to cultivate peas, it is important to know that the plants have support, which may be acquired at a plant supply store or nursery in the form of a stake or support. Peas require frequent watering and careful monitoring for weeds. Too many weeds will soon damage your pea crop, so weed them frequently and carefully.

Turnips

These are other quick-growing vegetables. Turnips can be eaten raw, roasted, boiled, or mashed. The only thing you need to remember when growing turnips is to water them frequently, as turnips require a lot of water to grow and flourish.

Corn

If you have space, corn is an excellent vegetable to grow. Corn that has been roasted or grilled is an excellent accompaniment to any meal, and watching a corn crop grow is an incredible sight. Additionally, the corn stalks can be composted afterward.

When you are growing corn, it is recommended to space the seeds at least 15 inches apart so they can grow conveniently.

When seeds are first planted, and again after two weeks, ensure that they are adequately treated with compost. After the first silks develop, you may begin enjoying your fresh organic corn.

Beets

Beets Always ensure that there is enough mulch down to keep the soil warm in the cool months and cool in the summer while producing beets. Ensure that you harvest all of your beets prior to the first frost.

Potatoes

Potato seeds are simple to plant and even simpler to cultivate. For optimal results, weed and hoe frequently, and plant them in bigger organic gardens. Potatoes help deter some insects, and children like digging potatoes in the fall.

Carrots

Carrots will grow as long as the soil is loose and deep enough.

Carrots grown organically are an excellent complement to any garden.

Green Beans

Planting green beans can help you save money if you are a parent or someone who frequently purchases canned green beans. Green beans can be planted immediately after the cold weather passes, with no risk of the ground freezing or the plants dying.

You can buy seeds that will grow in bushes or against a pole or stake. Pole green beans are typically easier to plant in smaller gardens.

Lettuce

Lettuce is easy and necessary to have if you're a salad eater. There are numerous varieties, and lettuce should be planted before the weather becomes excessively warm. Summer heat may rapidly wilt your lettuce, but during the cool spring months, your lettuce will grow well.

Radish

Radishes are another excellent salad plant and should be one of the first vegetables that a beginning organic grower should consider. They are simple to cultivate and can be grown throughout the summer and fall.

The Spring Onions

Spring onions are simple to plant because they require little water to flourish. They make an excellent garnish for any dish, and growing onions around the perimeter of your garden will help deter pests and give you good produce.

CHAPTER 5
PLANTING YOUR VEGETABLE GARDEN

After you've gathered all of your supplies and determined what to grow, it's time to plant your garden. Before you grab a shovel and run into your yard to begin digging, you may want to spend some time planning out your garden's layout.

Before you start digging up random holes in your garden, you should have a strong concept of what you want to plant and precisely where you want to place it.

The most effective technique to organize your garden is to take out a piece of paper and draw up a strategy for it. Determine the location of your garden and ensure that it is in an area that receives the majority of the day's sun. Begin studying your yard a few weeks before you begin planting, around when you begin building your compost pits. Make a note of which regions of your yard receive the majority of the day's sunlight and which portions of your lawn are frequently in the shade.

There are more considerations to consider while deciding where to plant your garden. Avoid locations that have just been repaired or are in close proximity to metal fences.

Substances like chemicals, metal and other debris may contaminate the environment, which may infect your plants. Additionally, keep an eye out for spots that hold water following a storm. The last thing you want to do is plant your garden in a location that will become a stagnant pool of water after each rain or irrigation. Once you've identified a suitable spot, immediately cease applying any chemicals on or near it.

When determining how to plant your seeds, aim at efficiency over aesthetics. If you're planting beans or peas alongside corn, line up the peas in front of the corn. In this manner, you may utilize the corn stalks as stakes rather than purchasing stakes for your plants. Additionally, to aid with pest control, consider planting onions, garlic, and herbs such as basil in a border around your vegetables. These fragrant vegetables will keep some insects away from your vegetables and also save your crops from being destroyed.

When you've chosen a location for your garden, proceed to your yard and remove any rocks or plants that are already growing there. Once all large boulders have been removed from the surface, remove all plants and then dig up a few inches of soil to loosen it. Dig/loosen an area around eight inches thick to create a decent working area.

Ascertain that the space you begin with is not excessively large. You want to start small and then expand as you gain experience with organic gardening and a better understanding of which crops to grow more of.

After removing any garbage from the chosen location and amending the soil, cover your garden site with a thick layer of organic mulch. This can include leaves from removed plants, dried grass from your yard, needles from trees, bark from trees, and other organic stuff. Assure that you do not use weeds or any substance that may carry weed seeds, such as hay. If you are reusing materials from a neighbor's property or another place, ensure that they have never been exposed to chemicals or pesticides. With these steps, you will have good results.

Following that, thinly spread the compost from your compost pits throughout the garden. By doing so, you're providing a nutrient-dense environment for your crops to develop. Combine soil from your back yard or even soil from beneath adjacent trees with this layer of compost until you have a few inches of soil and compost that is deep enough for planting.

When you're ready to plant your seeds, keep the soil moist but not soggy, and avoid trampling on it or compacting it in any other way. When you are ready, begin planting your seeds in the order that you previously determined. Pay close attention to the seed instructions about seed spacing and ensure that the seeds are sown slightly beneath the soil surface.

If this is your first time planting or you are concerned about seed spacing, create furrows by putting a layer of soil aside and then consider producing your own seed tape.

If you have toilet paper and a spray bottle capable of spraying water, you are set. Simply roll the toilet paper out on a table, sprinkle it with the sprayer, and scatter the seeds according to the guidelines on the seed packets.

Cover the seeds with a second long strip of toilet paper, fold the edges, then spray it once more to ensure the seeds remain in place. Then, take the seed tape out to your garden and insert it into the furrows you've already prepared, covering it with soil. This will save you time outside determining the proper spacing between seeds and subsequently worrying about the potential of planting the seeds too close together.

Another way to plant seeds is to purchase pre-started seeds. This indicates that the seeds have begun to sprout. Seeds that have already sprouted are typically available at garden centers, and many organic seeds come in biodegradable packaging. Once you've received the seeds, all you need to do is put the pots in your garden area, then wrap the sprouts in old newspaper and cover them with mulch. This method works very fine.

You can also start seeds at home and save money by using your own containers and compost from your compost pile. By beginning seeds, you will allow them to sprout, usually inside with the assistance of a grow light, before transplanting them to a garden. It is best to start organic seeds in biodegradable containers to avoid the damage that can occur during transplantation. After the seeds sprout, simply plant the containers in your garden, enclosing them with newspaper and mulch.

If you are directly seeding the seeds into the ground or planting by hand, laying down the mulch and newspaper can be a pain. Indeed, it will likely be the most challenging aspect of your new garden, as you want to avoid covering your seeds. Marking your seeds as you plant them or waiting until the seeds have begun to sprout is usually the easiest approach to avoid difficulty.

It is advised that you immediately mark the seed places and lay mulch. while this is an additional effort, it will be well worth it because the newspaper and mulch will aid in water retention and discourage weed development and insect infestations. This will also preserve your crop until the time of harvest.

CHAPTER 6
MAKING YOUR GARDEN THRIVE

Many individuals are tempted to sit back and wait for their garden to bloom after the seeds have been planted. These individuals feel that after the seeds are planted, all of the hard work is complete and nothing further has to be done. While it may be tempting to sit back and enjoy the results of your labor, you must remember that work must continue if you want your organic vegetable garden to expand and thrive.

Organic Gardening Tips and Guides For Beginners

The first and most important thing to remember is to water your plants daily. If you have a family, this might be a shared family chore that children or spouses can take turns doing. Many people use watering the garden as an excuse to get outside and enjoy the beautiful weather during the spring and early summer. On rainy days, you do not need to worry about watering your garden, but be sure that the change in routine does not cause you to forget to water the next day, once the rain has ceased.

Watering the garden in the morning should be done. If at all feasible, before 10:00am. If you wait until the afternoon, the hot noon heat will frequently evaporate the water before it has a chance to properly water your young plants. While watering your plants, keep an eye on the mulch to ensure it does not become too matted. This may result in the seeds being deprived of water.

Matted mulch can compact and absorb the water applied to your plants.

Overwatering your garden is something you must avoid at all costs! This has occurred to a number of naive gardeners, particularly if the garden is located in a home with multiple would-be gardeners. It is simple for two or more household members to water the garden simultaneously.

To avoid this, communicate with your neighbors and ensure that no one has watered the garden prior to going out to water it. Additionally, while out in the garden, check to see if the ground is too moist or soggy, which could indicate recent irrigation.

Excessive watering eventually drowns plants and can be just as detrimental as insufficient irrigation.

Keep note of the amount of water your garden receives and, following a heavy rainstorm, you may want to wait a day or two before watering the vegetables again. After a heavy rainstorm, examine the garden to determine whether the soil is still highly wet and avoid watering the vegetable garden if the soil remains highly saturated.

Your ultimate goal should be to water consistently. If you share watering tasks with others, establish a timetable to control when gardens are watered and, if possible, the amount of water used. Consistently watering your plants at the same time each day with the same amount of water will work miracles.

Weeding is another critical aspect of growing organic vegetables that many novice gardeners ignore. Weeds easily take over a vegetable garden, destroying the vegetables and leaving you with an overgrown garden. Each day, inspect your garden for weeds and eliminate them as soon as you discover them.

Due to the fact that you are growing an organic garden, you cannot use enticing weed sprays or chemicals. Rather than that, you should rely on traditional hoeing and weed pulling. If your garden is thoroughly inspected each day, it is possible to pull weeds quickly and efficiently before they grow out of control. Weeding is another duty that is beneficial to rotate, particularly when youngsters are involved. When we were children, many of our grandparents spent hours carefully weeding their family gardens by hand as punishment for some mischief.

Insects are another concern when growing an organic garden. While some insects and "pests" are beneficial for garden growth, an excessive number will devour your vegetables before your family has a chance to harvest anything. Mulch and newspaper will help control insects, slugs, and other common garden pests, but insects will frequently persist. The following are some of the insects that all organic gardeners should be on the lookout for, along with some methods for eradicating them:

Corn Earworm: These insects can be avoided all together by working the soil during the spring and fall to expose the pupae. Exposing them will lead to them being destroyed by wind and rain or predators. If you notice caterpillars spray them with diluted soapy water and homemade insecticide.

Cutworm: An easy way to get rid of these pests is to spread wheat bran and molasses over garden beds a week before planting new plants. There are also nematodes that can be added to the soil to destroy the cutworm or you (or your children) can pick the caterpillars off each evening once the sun has gone down. The full night is often the best time to catch them and do this.

Cabbage Worm: If you see these worms while the caterpillars are still little, you can spray them with diluted soapy water or homemade insecticide. Once they have grown, they can also be plucked off by hand. Another task for your children, or children in your community that enjoys playing with insects and caterpillars.

Tomato Hornworm: While the caterpillars are still small, spray them with a homemade insecticide, and till the soil in the fall to help eliminate any surviving pupae. If there are only a handful, they can be readily picked off by hand.

Slugs and snails: These are the scourge of most organic gardens. Many people invest in expensive raised plant beds in the hopes of completely avoiding snails and slugs, but there are less expensive alternatives to avoid both snails and slugs. The first method is to use copper tape to outline your garden area. Growing clover attracts natural predators, which attach the snails and slugs while leaving your garden alone. Finally, you can use shallow pans of beer to catch them in and around your garden. Every day, dispose of all slugs and snails trapped in this manner.

Aphids: These insects are typically repelled by diluted soapy water or even plain water. If your plants are badly affected in some locations, clip off these leaves and dispose of them as soon as possible.

Flea Beetle: Beneficial nematodes can be put into the soil to help remove these and other similar insects. Row coverings can also be utilized to cover and protect the plants when possible. One fantastic approach to prevent these pests entirely is to plant your crops later in the spring after the main population of flea beetles have either moved out of your area (ideally) or been attracted to existing gardens.

Cucumber beetle: Nematodes, like flea beetles, will help eliminate these beetles. Once they have matured or appeared in your garden, they can be plucked off or sprayed with a homemade insecticide. Once you've brought in your crop, make sure to clean up the garden space to avoid a new infestation during the next growing season.

Squash Bug: These bugs may often be found hiding on the undersides of your leaves, so keep an eye out for them in your garden. When you spot them, you can pick them off. If it does not keep them at bay, you should spray the plants with a homemade insecticide.

If insects have taken over your organic vegetable garden, there are a few things you can do to help them go. Making your own organic insecticide is one approach to help get rid of insects. Take two teaspoons of dish liquid soap and combine it with one cup of vegetable oil to make this. Mix a couple of teaspoons of this combination with water in a spray bottle and spray the most highly damaged portions of your garden.

If spraying isn't working, consider growing natural repellent plant borders around your vegetables if you haven't previously. If there is adequate space, insect repellent plants can be placed in between the rows of crops, and they can be much more effective than homemade bug spray. Onions and garlic are two vegetables that are excellent insect repellents, and herbs such as basil can also aid. These plants are frequently available in small pots that are already half-grown and ready to be placed into your garden to provide immediate protection.

In addition to insects, organic vegetable growers must keep an eye out for a variety of other things. A healthy vegetable garden can be destroyed by funguses and other plant diseases before it has a chance to truly thrive. Look for inexplicable wilting, molding, rotting, blotches, moldy coatings, whiting, rusting, and spots when looking for plant diseases.

It is far easier to prevent certain diseases than it is to treat them, and taking proper care of your vegetable garden is essential. Each year, rotate your crops and keep the growing area clean in-between seasons. Always keep your crops well watered and fertilized when growing them, as this will help them stay healthy.

Look for disease-resistant seeds and plants, as well as disease-free seedlings. The following is a list of the most common plant illnesses that will assist you in diagnosing and treating them organically:

Bacterial Leaf Spot: This is a prevalent problem in some gardens, and it's something that many new organic gardeners may notice right away. Small, black, or brown water-soaked patches will appear on leaves affected by this disease. The infected leaves will typically drop off and die early when the spots dry up, break, and leave holes.

Tomatoes, peppers, and cabbage family members are all susceptible to this illness. The symptoms will most likely occur during wet weather and can be controlled by removing contaminated leaves as soon as possible. It can be difficult to keep up with the sickness in the rain, but it is possible.

Late blight is a disease that primarily affects tomatoes and potatoes later in the growing season. The illness will first appear as damp grayish or greenish patches on the leaves, then proceed to a white fungal growth on the undersides of the leaves. There are various disease-resistant tomato and potato varieties on the market. When these kinds become available, choose them regardless of cost since you will get the benefits of a higher yield. If you can't identify a resistant type, remove and discard any infected plant parts. One technique to help prevent this disease is to water plants first thing in the morning so that they can dry completely during the day, preventing fungus growth.

Common Rust: Rust can affect a variety of vegetables, so it's important to keep an eye out for it. Asparagus, corn, and onions are among the most typically impacted vegetables.

A reddish-brown patch that seems powdery is the most typical indication of common rust.

These spots typically form on the leaves of the susceptible vegetables and rub off when touched. The spread of infection can be slowed by selecting contaminated leaves by hand. Plants that are severely diseased should be removed and destroyed totally.

There are techniques to entirely avoid typical rust. One technique is to ensure that all plants have adequate air circulation. Avoid planting seeds too close together, as this can result in overcrowding. Also, weed your garden frequently and prune your plants to ensure that they are properly disseminated.

Anthracnose

Organic vegetable gardeners in the United States will encounter anthracnose more frequently than growers in other nations. This disease affects the stems, leaves, and fruits of the plants in warm, moist areas.

The vegetables that are most commonly afflicted by the disease are cucumbers, tomatoes, melons, and beans.

Small spots will appear on various areas of the affected vegetables at first. Pink spores will form in the center of the spots later. Spraying water with a little lime juice on the leaf buds will help prevent the disease from developing or spreading. Any severely contaminated plants must be removed and destroyed completely.

Virus Mosaic

This illness is very infectious and, if not treated properly, can infect an entire garden. Although there is now no cure for this virus, there are plants and seeds available that are already immune to it. The illness is identified by the affected plants' growth is stunted and their leaves curling for no apparent cause. Infected plants must be eradicated, and spraying plants with homemade pesticides to kill or repel any insects carrying the virus is one technique to help reduce the disease's chances.

Wilts is another disease that can spread across your garden. Lower leaves wilt and are often accompanied by yellow spots, making them easy to spot. To completely avoid the disease, organic vegetable growers should keep an eye out for disease-carrying cucumber beetles and other insects. Planting disease-resistant plants is also a good idea for vegetable growers.

Powdery Mildew

This disease will affect the leaves, stalks, and blossoms of your garden crops. It appears as powdery mildew that leaves a white or gray coating on the affected areas. Pruning plants to increase air circulation and removing any fallen leaves from underneath the plants are two ways to avoid mildew. Baking soda can be used to cure the condition and prevent it from spreading if you keep organic mulch around your plants. Baking soda mixed with water and sprayed on diseased plants will help them heal and prevent further infections.

Clubroot

A fungus that lives in the soil infects the clubroot of cabbage, cauliflower, and broccoli. Plants affected by this disease will have swollen roots and wilt in direct sunlight. Purchasing disease-resistant seeds and rotating vegetable crops each year are two ways to avoid clubroot.

After you've defeated weeds, insects, and disease-causing water shortages, you must always ensure that your vegetables are getting adequate nutrients. This nutrient is obtained from the fertile soil and compost in which they are developing. To encourage development, don't be scared to apply more compost around your growing plants.

Some plants, such as corn, require compost every few weeks in order to thrive. Consider getting organic manure from local nurseries and even small farms if you feel your compost isn't making enough of an impact. Although aged manure may sound revolting, it can make the difference between a healthy, growing garden and one that is struggling.

CHAPTER 7
HANDLING YOUR ORGANIC VEGETABLES

You've started your own organic vegetable garden by planting it and doing everything you can to get it started. Unfortunately, the seeds have not yet sprouted, or the seeds that have sprouted have not grown much, if at all. There are a few things you should attempt before you throw in the towel and give up on organic gardening.

First and foremost, have you been hand weeding your garden on a daily basis? This may appear to be a tedious and insignificant task, yet it could make all the difference in the world. Make a habit of visiting your vegetable garden on a daily basis and thoroughly inspecting it for weeds. Do not let your children do it, and do not rely on a glimpse out your back window to determine whether or not weeds are growing.

Many gardeners have done a cursory inspection and discovered that the sprouts they believed were sprouting in their garden were actually weeds. Each day, conduct a comprehensive inspection and weed by hand to ensure that the job is completed completely. Throw these weeds away, not into your compost pile. To achieve the greatest results, devote 20 minutes per day to weeding.

If you've been weeding your garden every day and your plants are still developing slowly, try adding rich, aged, and compost to the slow-growing vegetables. Many plants simply require assistance, and other vegetables, such as corn, pumpkins, and squash, require compost to add richness and nutrition. Spreading some aged compost from your compost pits will aid in the growth of your vegetables.

If applying compost to your vegetables every few days yields no benefits, consider purchasing some manure from your local garden supply store. They will frequently have organic manure available for your gardening requirements, which will work as a more potent fertilizer than compost. If you are hesitant to use manure, you might start with some aged compost purchased from a nursery. In many circumstances, your compost pits will be only a few weeks old when you try to use them to foster growth, so some older compost may suffice.

Don't be hesitant to increase the amount of water you give your garden. You want to avoid overwatering your plants, but you also want to ensure that they get enough water to survive and develop. Always check to see if the soil appears dry before watering your plants in the morning. If the soil appears to be dry one day after watering, you may want to increase the amount of water you give them.

Around your plants, the earth should always be slightly damp.

Finally, don't be scared to spray your plants with your homemade pesticide or even diluted soapy water to get rid of insects. If your vegetable garden attracts a lot of pests, consider spraying once every ten days or once every two weeks. Spray diluted soapy water straight over vegetables that are constantly infested with insects.

CHAPTER 8
HOW TO HARVEST ORGANIC VEGETABLES

The finest part of having an organic garden is usually harvesting your organic crops. Even if only one or two members of the family have really assisted throughout the growing season, the entire family will normally volunteer to help. The harvest time for your organic vegetables varies by plant, with many crops ripening throughout the season.

It's critical to harvest your vegetables as soon as they're ready, rather than allowing them to sit in the sun. If left out after ripening, many vegetables will quickly degrade and lose flavor. They will also become overly mushy and delicate, losing all of their attractiveness.

Some plants can be left out after they've ripened or even harvested before they've fully matured. The following is a list of widely produced vegetables in organic gardens and their harvest periods. Check your gardens frequently around harvest time, as certain vegetables will ripen in a matter of hours. Keep inspecting your garden even after you've taken in a significant crop since some plants simply produce additional vegetables after the first crop is removed.

Beets

Beets should be harvested when the diameter is between 14 and 2 inches and the leaves are 4 to 6 inches long. Remember that the tops of the beets can be eaten as well!

Beans

Snap beans should be harvested when the pods are firm and snap readily, and the seeds are still immature.

Carrots

Carrots should be picked when they are crisp and have a diameter of 12 to 1 inch. Younger carrots are more sensitive, but older carrots are usually sweeter, so you can wait until the first frost to harvest them. If you like younger carrots, harvest them as soon as they reach maturity and grow more for a fresh crop.

Corn

Corn should be harvested when the silk begins to darken and shrivel. This happens roughly 20 days after the first silk strands appear, but it can happen sooner, so keep a watch out.

Cucumbers

Cucumbers should be harvested when they are between 2 and 8 inches long, depending on your preferences. When they're dark green, firm, and crisp, they're ready to eat. Keep an eye on the cucumbers after they've been removed since others will grow in their place.

Eggplant

When eggplant is 6 to 8 inches long and shiny with rich color, it is ready to harvest. To remove the fruit from the plant, use pruning shears or a knife.

Garlic

When the tops of the bulbs start to turn yellow and dry up, it's time to harvest garlic. Before storing the bulbs, they must be dried on screens, with the roots near to the bulbs being trimmed and the loose outer sheaths being removed.

Onions

In the fall, loosen the soil, pull out the roots, and cut off the roots to harvest spring onions and leeks.

Lettuce

Lettuce can be harvested 50 to 60 days after sowing. They can usually be harvested when they are young, but they will reach their full size in 60 days.

Okra

When okra pods are young and sensitive, harvest them. Allow the pods to grow no longer than 3 inches in length. More pods will develop once you select them, and you'll have to harvest them every day.

Onions

After the tops of the onions have fallen off, harvest them. Allow the onions to air dry for two days after digging them up.

Peas

Peas should be harvested when the pods are green and plump yet still sensitive. A week after the plant flowers, the pods are usually ready to harvest.

Peppers

When peppers are ready, they can be harvested at any size or left to develop more for a greater flavor.

Potatoes

Using a spading fork, harvest large potatoes after the vine has died. The potatoes are usually four to six inches below the soil surface and must be handled with care to avoid bruising and spoilage.

Pumpkins

Pumpkins should only be harvested after they have fully ripened on the vines, and before the first hard freeze. The rind should be firm and uniformly colored.

Radishes

Radishes should be harvested when they reach the size of large marbles and no larger than 1 inch in diameter.

Squash

When the squash plant is between 6 and 8 inches in diameter, it's time to harvest it. They're ready to harvest 4 to 8 weeks after the plant blooms.

Turnips

Turnips are ready to harvest when the roots are 2 to 3 inches in diameter and the tops are 4 to 6 inches long. The tips can also be eaten.

It may seem stupid to follow vegetable harvesting instructions, but if you do not harvest your vegetables in the precise time range, you will be unable to use them later. Don't throw away all of your hard work. Pay special attention to when you plant your vegetables and inspect them frequently as the harvest approaches.

Vegetables that require thinning or frequent harvesting should be harvested once a day or every other day by you or a family member. If you don't harvest your vegetables on a regular basis, the plants will quickly grow dormant. If you'll be using and eating these vegetables frequently, only plant vegetables like peas and squash that will continue to ripen after the initial crop are picked to avoid becoming overworked.

If you don't think you'll be able to keep track of the appropriate harvest seasons or if you don't think you'll be able to harvest huge quantities of vegetables, cultivate just vegetables like peppers that are forgiving when it comes to harvesting on time. Consider growing turnips if you live in a chilly climate where frosts occur frequently. Turnips may be left in the ground safely even after a strong frost and dug up well into the winter.

CHAPTER 9
HOW TO STORE YOUR ORGANIC VEGETABLES

You might be unsure what to do with your vegetables once they've been harvested. Even a large family will struggle to eat enough fresh organic vegetables on a regular basis. Keeping your vegetables in your home will help you prevent wasting them.

Although some vegetables are more easily kept than others, most organic vegetables may be stored and saved in some fashion.

There are a variety of ways to store your crop, so don't be discouraged if you've grown more than you can consume. Many grocery stores sell mason jars and other ingredients for preparing preserves and canning vegetables, as well as how-to instructions. Cheesecloth is available at the same locations, and it's perfect for drying vegetables if you're air-drying them.

Along with your oven, food dehydrators can be used to dry your vegetables. When drying vegetables in an oven, put them to the lowest temperature, usually 140 degrees, and keep an eye on them to make sure they are drying rather than roasting.

Lettuce

When you've finished harvesting all of your lettuce, wash it, remove the core, and dry it with a towel. When you're done, place it in a plastic bag in the crisper portion of your refrigerator. Your lettuce will stay crisp for up to a week if you do this.

Because it is more difficult to keep vegetables for an extended amount of time, it is best to pick your lettuce and begin utilizing it before it has reached full growth. Use what you can, keep what you can, and give the remainder to friends and family after it has reached full development. They'll be grateful for some organic salad to use in their salads or on their sandwiches.

Vegetables with Roots

As long as root vegetables are gathered on time and appropriately, they can store for longer than other vegetables. Check to see if any of your vegetables have been bruised or damaged throughout the harvesting process. If they've been tampered with, toss them out since rotting may quickly spread if you're not careful.

Many root vegetables, such as potatoes, carrots, sweet potatoes, and others, can be stored in a cool, dark, dry location, such as a root cellar or pantry. Other root vegetables, such as carrots, can be dried in a food dehydrator or even in a low-heat oven. Some vegetables, such as turnips, can be stored in the crisper of a refrigerator, especially if they will be used soon.

Tomatoes

There are a variety of ways to store tomatoes, which is great because tomatoes are a favorite of many organic gardeners. If tomatoes are still a little green, they can be stored on a countertop or on a window sill. They can be kept in the refrigerator as well.

Some people dry tomatoes or even store them for later use in sauces. Tomato preserves, whether sweet with ripened tomatoes or pickle with green tomatoes, can be a tasty winter treat.

Onions

Onions will stay in any dry, dark spot for a long time. The onions can be stored in a pantry or attic for a long period if they are not bruised and show no signs of dampness.

Peas and Beans

Peas and Beans may usually be harvested as needed, but when it comes time to store them, there are a few options. Peas and beans can be kept in the refrigerator for several days in bags. With the right equipment, they can also be canned. Beans can also be dried, which is a common method of storage. Beans can be soaked and cooked after they have been dried and bagged.

Corn

Corn may be kept in the refrigerator or frozen for a long time once the husk has been removed.

You can also dry, preserve, and cream the kernels at a later time.

CONCLUSION

I'm sure you gained a lot of knowledge from this book. I'd like you to know that anyone can conduct organic vegetable gardening at home because the principles are similar to those used on the farm. The main difference is that you operate in a smaller space and have more freedom in terms of plant selection.

The first step is to identify a suitable place. Many people cultivate organic food gardens in their backyards. To make it work, make sure that whatever you're planting gets at least 6 hours of sunlight each day and that it has access to water.

You should do the same as the ancient civilizations who relied on an efficient irrigation system by ensuring enough drainage because if you don't, you'll have to undertake organic vegetable farming in a raised bed.

It's time to develop the land once you've located your ideal place. To pull out the weeds on the ground, you'll need your gardening equipment and a pair of gloves. It may take many days to ensure that the place is ready for planting.

Only by testing the ground where you intend to plant your produce and mixing it with the soil will you be able to tell if it is a good site. If it is able to integrate and consolidate itself with the soil, you may begin planting your vegetables and watch them flourish over the coming weeks.

You can produce your own compost using coffee grounds, dead leaves, grass clippings, food waste, or even manure if you don't want to buy it from the garden store. They're also fantastic fertilizers.

When it comes to your vegetables, keep in mind that some of them may not be appropriate for the soil you're putting them on. This is due to a number of circumstances outside your control, including weather, pests, and other plant-borne diseases. You may avoid making this error by doing some research and asking other organic gardeners about what crops are best to plant in your location.

Planting a variety of organic vegetables at once is one approach to protect them against pests, as some of them defend each other from bugs. Crop rotation is a term used to describe a process that allows you to adapt to the weather in your location. Another effective protection technique is to enlist the support of Mother Nature, which has proven to be beneficial in the form of birds, insects, and even toads.

If you live in a region where wild animals are likely to consume your vegetables, you should install fences to keep them out. Animal hair, baby powder, and deodorant soaps are some other options.

Weed removal is a part of the land preparation process. However, keep in mind that new weeds will emerge after some time, so you'll need to monitor the area on a regular basis.

Planting your own organic vegetable garden at home would undoubtedly save you money, as organic vegetables are fairly costly in supermarkets. If you have any extra stocks when it's time to harvest them, you may either give them to your neighbors or sell them at the local market for a profit, which isn't terrible given that you didn't spend a lot of money on this investment.

Thank you for taking the time to read this.

WRITE YOUR REVIEW

I believe you enjoyed this book and also learned a lot. Kindly go to the comment section of the website where you purchased this book and leave your honest review. I will really appreciate your feedback.

OTHER BOOKS BY ANN WILLIVAN

There are other books written by me,

"ANN WILLIVAN"

Check them out.

Thanks For Reading.

Cheers.

Note

Note

Note

Note

Note